Axis Mundi

Axis Mundi

POEMS

KAREN HOLMBERG

John Ciardi Prize for Poetry Winner
Selected by Lorna Dee Cervantes

BkMk Press
University of Missouri-Kansas City

BkMk Press
University of Missouri-Kansas City
5101 Rockhill Road
Kansas City, Missouri 64110
(816) 235-2558 (voice)
(816) 235-2611 (fax)
www.umkc.edu/bkmk

Financial assistance for this project has been provided by the Missouri Arts Council, a state agency.

Cover and Section Page Art: John Digby
Author Photo: Shannon Bedford
Book design: Susan L. Schurman
Managing Editor: Ben Furnish
Associate Editor: Michelle Boisseau
Executive Editor: Robert Stewart

The John Ciardi Prize for Poetry wishes to thank Curtis Bauer, Lindsey Martin-Bowen, Susan Cobin, Steve Gehrke, Elaine K. Lally, and Linda Rodriguez.

BkMk Press wishes to thank Linda D. Brennaman, Brandi Handley, Samantha Martin, Marie McKim Mayhugh, Pamela Rasch, Gregory Van Winkle.

Printing: Sheridan Books

Library of Congress Cataloging-in-Publication Data

Holmberg, Karen E., 1966-
 Axis mundi : poems / Karen Holmberg. -- 1st ed.
    p. cm.
 Includes bibliographical references.
 "Winner of the John Ciardi Prize for Poetry selected by Lorna Dee Cervantes."
 ISBN 978-1-886157-83-5
 I. Title.
 PS3558.O3573A95 2012
 811'.54--dc23

                    2012029645

This book is set in Garamond Premier Pro and Baker Signet.

ACKNOWLEDGMENTS

My gratitude goes to the editors who chose to publish the following poems, and whose suggestions often improved them:

Blueline: "Axis." *Cave Wall*: "Imago," "The Flash Phenomenon," "The Sheen Remains." *Cimarron Review*: "Still Life with Yews." *Cold Mountain Review*: "The Keeper." *Comstock Review*: "Sweetbriar." *Connecticut Review*: "Axis Mundi." *Hotel Amerika*: "Obeisance." *Hunger Mountain*: "The Slug." *New Madrid*: "Garnet, the Poor Man's Ruby," "Salvage." *Nimrod*: "Pear Tree." *Poetry East*: "Nettles," "Study with Bark, Stones, Leaves, and Mother." *Potomac Review*: "Ward." *Quarterly West*: "Box Turtle," "Soft-shell Crab," "The Aerialist" (as part of a series "Reflections on Home"). *Shenandoah*: "Zebra Finch at Petco." *Southern Poetry Review*: "Living Fossil," "*Do You Breathe*," "Ephemeroptera" (as "Ephemerata"). "Living Fossil" was reprinted in the 10 year anniversary issue of *Southern Poetry Review*. *Subtropics*: "First Word." *Terrain.org*: "Exchange of Azalea and Quail," "The Model Plane," "To the Ox Netsuke in the Flea Market." *The Healing Muse*: "Sutures," "Negative." *The Spoon River Poetry Review*: "Something Hard under the Skin." *West Branch*: "Surrogate," "Dislocation of the Thumb," "Pessary." "Ephemeroptera," "The Aerialist," "Soft-Shell Crab," "Sutures," and "Living Fossil" appear on *Fishhouse, www.fishousepoems.org*. "Ward" and "Imago" appear on *Oregon Poetic Voices, http://oregonpoeticvoices.org/*. "Imago" appeared in the *Hecht Prize Anthology*.

I am also grateful to the following organizations which provided time, space, and support to write these poems: Susquehanna University; Oregon State University's Center for the Humanities, Horning Support Program for Humanistic Scholarship, and Spring Creek Project. I would also like to thank the Soapstone Foundation and Centrum for the restorative solitude of their residency programs. My students have been models of persistence and the venturesome spirit; without them I would be unmoored. I am indebted to Penelope Pelizzon for commenting on multiple drafts and radically improving this work. I also would like to thank Michelle Boisseau for opening up routes for reentry and revision. I have never adequately thanked Nancy Paschuk for her compassion and stories, and for reminding me that poetry can shape rituals for almost any need; many of these poems began in her office. To Aria, Ava, and Lily: deep gratitude for giving each day the intensity of passionate love.

AXIS MUNDI

FOREWORD

This delicate web of words holds strong as spider silk. "Nothing is exactly as it seems, nor is it otherwise," said Zen master, T'sai Ken T'an, and the same is true of this collection. Each line is packed and shimmers with sense, resonating and reverberating past the poet, past the poem and past this world as it is. It draws us past death itself with its final silence in the continuing echo. Grief holds this book to its core as gravity holds us to this earth, it grounds us from lightning strike, it makes something from nothing—becomes the axis mundi, that point of contact between upper and lower worlds which makes us more human.

This subtle collection is hardly dark or grim. Bristling with insights, each poem does a deft dance between line-break and poetic image. As in all great poetry, it allows us to "see" the ordinary. Jonquils are real flowers in an actual garden, the yew is just yew—until she becomes the ghost of Sylvia Plath in the moonlight; we are present in the poem to the scents, to the velvet, slick or prickle of their touch while at the same time they become something else entirely. Shards of "minute particulars" take us into the archeology of the sacred and profane moments which happen all at once, always already.

This book will make you feel as it acts upon the senses in the way a certain African fruit will flavor everything sweet by neutralizing the sour and negating the bitter. Here are full and breathtakingly well-crafted poems worthy of the name, John Ciardi.

Lorna Dee Cervantes
Final Judge, John Ciardi Prize for Poetry

To my daughters, Ava and Lily

Axis

What got me about the trees today
           was how a breadth of field refined
the hoopla of their fall
           to fanfare: snow of high karat
swerved to a funnel, tinged rose by sundown's
           globed fire.

           I walked and looked, and looked until I found
I was in it, and could see
           the singular careen of
a sycamore leaf, a stiffened velveteen
           whose lobe tips curled
like the bows of gondolas.

Spinning, spinning without
           resistance: gay and stately as a carousel
with the grace of things
           of gravity aloft.
As it fell, the idea rose
           through it

           as when a choir descends
the whole tone scale, and floats
           the overtone's gossamer tent.
Faint scuff on asphalt, absolute rest:
           a beauty so bare my eyes closed
involuntarily round it.

i

Ward

When the East is gold leaf beaten so thin
the sky's pale violet shows through, I go
to my garden to check the progress
of its labors. The peony's fist
has widened its fissure in earth.
I stoop to assist, unkinking
its wrist, unfolding the wad of maroon tissues
snipped with half-moons, triangles, and blades.
      Partly in pity, in part for relief,
the world gave me
two daughters to distract me from
my own death dread, that I might relax my hold
on her, the way you give a baby
the transparent nipple, the vinyl infant
to mother. When the nurse handed me
my first, I kissed the lip curled
in a sob of dismay, already possessed.
Then I rolled back the sleeve of her gown
and saw fingers wizened from being
too long in the bag of waters,
unfurled the fist to find
a shredded blister in her palm, slits
in the whitened, drowned skin revealing
tissues so thin they took their color
from blood, the palm lines
a crimson *M* as if gouged with a stick.
      How privileged
I was in that maternity ward, able to believe
the distance of her death, that I could keep
for life what had entered the world
through my body's gates. That it would never be
my temple and cheek grinding the sand,
my teeth bared in agony near the small hand,

the palm still enfolding loosely
the stripped twig, the skin of the fingers livid, abraded,
taken to great age in a single day
by the mother who gives to us, and gives to us,
then wrenches away what we love
in her vast wave.

Box Turtle

Retracted in the folds of your throat's
                    side-pleat-exploded
change purse, two nostrils nest,
            pores precise, slightly lipped as if
tooth-picked in clay. You're

a moated fortress, plastron drawn up
                    drawbridge-style. But after
twenty minutes jolting at my hip
            you figure no good ever comes
of abduction, and extend your beak

just far enough for me to look
                    into wary eyes, tiny domes
ground of gold and green
            glass chunks, blood-flecked
as an old alcoholic's. Your pale tongue,

plump and dry, conducts
                    a buzzing chord, imperative
as a dial tone. I set you down to complete
            your call, moved by how you trump
my own persistence with that primal *now*.

First Word

Gone rigid-kneed, imperious, her hips
magnetically repel the car seat, leaping back

each time I try to settle her and latch
her in. Then I see

she's pointing over my shoulder.
Moon, she says urgently, then more reflective

moon, *moon*, the *m* and *n*
taut as skin around the vowel's

gravid solemnity. I turn in time
to see the amber disk unlip a ridge

whose pelt of trees gleams
dully like a bar of charcoal. It simmers

somehow, a granular brilliance
plasma-slick, like a cell just healed

from the dividing. Rising behind a maple's
ruddy crown, its flood of light restores

to thinning, drought-exhausted leaves
a greenish life.

              Now the street lamps
flicker on and pour their interrogatory glare.

The pointing finger briefly swivels to these spots
that whirl with illusory snow of late-hatched

river midges. Yet, at fifteen months,
she already knows the false moons

from the true, and turns again, reaching
her upturned palm, fingers

curling, curling, as if to collect to herself
all those lumens.

Ephemeroptera

ephemeros— "short-lived"
pteron—"wing"

Consider mayflies, daughter-caught in Bonne
Maman jam jars, their wide variety:
wax white, slate green, with Day-Glo or popsicle
orange eyes, some with striped stockings on, or wagging
their filament tails like puppies. They've gone through
twenty nymphal stages in their stream, two years
clutching a lump of black-slimed chert
only to emerge with vestigial mouths,
to blizzard for two weeks round
the mercury lamps in the parking lot
of Val-U-City.

Consider all the allowances spent on
Mexican jumping beans, the hinged acrylic
case with magnifying lid placed lightly
as a grenade on the conveyer. Hand-warmed
the whole ride home they finally began
a little arrhythmic kick against your palm.
Consider the caterpillar's final task before she spins
the silk sac: to score a compass-perfect circle
so the moth she'll be can pop the hatch, escape
to lay her eggs in the ovary
of the Sebastiana flower that blooms
only in the Sonora's
blazing arroyos.

Consider change drastic and costly, things
coming from nothings all around us; consider that
the more urgent the business is,
the more ephemeral. Is it a wonder
we are tempted to wish
with a child's ardency, *Let this
creased and baggy garment
be cocoon!*

Living Fossil

Horseshoe Crab, Limulidae

Funereal
and everlasting:
   like the hundred and four year old
Old World relic in my family's
   album, propped
in broadcloth shellacked with wear
   in a shell-backed

rattan chair, seamed face pursed
   to an O.
         A museum plaque details
your vast immunities: you can fast
   a year, can abide
viscous salinities,
   antarcticas of cold. Nothing
taxes you to change;

   you've been granted for proper use,
benefit and behoof
   a spacious class between
the high-rise neighborhoods of arachnid
   and crustacean, and
life in perpetuity to boot.
   Turns out we've adapted you;

your blue antibacterial blood
   tests the purity of our drugs.
It's what we have to do
   to last. I find even I
have covenanted with you,
   absorbing your chitin
when my uterus was sutured.

How glad I am you've waited
three hundred million years to name
    an heir to your estate, when you
rejuvenate each June,
    clambering, being clambered aboard
in full-moon estuaries,
    your fencing foil

sparring, churning sperm among
    giant tapioca eggs. By fall
your foal-hoof young will moult
    and mulch the crisped eelgrass
with parchment miniatures,
    translucent, richly tender
as if carved of *plus gras* butter.

Soft-shell Crab

An odd infinitive, *to crab*, intention
    wavering like a spirit level's

bubble between ode
    and deed. Teaching my nieces

patience, I suppose. How some things must be
    taken unawares. That we can draw up

a mystery in fingerbreadths of string, or lure it
    toward counterfeit moons. Placing

the mesh between you and the depths
    you flee to, we scoop with a nimble wrist turn

as you shoot sidewise powered by delicate
    sculling oars, earning the Latin handle

Callinectes sapidus: beautiful swimmer.

    But not tonight; tonight you creep
with the rolling motion of blown thistledown

    into the net. Pulled into unbuoying air
you're a sodden giant, seven inches

    point to point. You've taken
rapid transit to doughy old age, all minerals

    of your hardened past retracted to the gem
of calcium you hold near your heart.

Cautious, we depress your shell, padded
as a damp cigar, the blackened green of bruised leaves.

We squeeze the flaccid threat of the opening claw,
and lay the throats of our fingers

on the pliable spines of that guillotine-to-be.

Dislocation of the Thumb

One of my vassals has finally slipped
the shackles. Shoots
like suckerwood off my wrist.
Has wandered,
the way the breast on a painted
quattrocento Virgin
can goiter her neck, or nestle
against her shoulder for her cheek to brood.
When the nurse unfastens
the ice-pack's diaper
my thumb becomes
the erection,
tingling, aching, nothing-doing,
on the baby boy I never had. Something
unretractable. A snail's
stuck eye.

The nurse settles
the gasmask's glutinous ring.
I suck and suck
and finally pull from its windpipe
an hysterical shriek
the way they need me to, so the doc
can soften the muscle's
green plum.
I laugh in the face of pain.
It is telling me
the only joke it knows, the one
that never falls flat. Then I hear
the distant, crisp,
and blessed snap on the stage
of my dark theatre—droplet

rejoined to me!—and doc offers
his arm off the gurney.
I fling my hot paw over
in mute appeal, recalling
my dog, inoperable
tumor bulging her eye,
even as her heart pulled to itself
the barbiturate's cooling flood.

The Slug

It glides by
with the grand leisure of a whale
in migration. Yet once it sees me
     it retires, melts a little
          foreskin over

     its face. The prompt
eyes probe upward and re-bloom, dewed
with humectants. I stroke its neck,
     glandular and chilled
          as a dog's nose.

     When I cover
the single nostril like a fife's
finger hole, the back contracts to buck
     me off in slo-mo.
          Or is time

     lapsing radically
when, under its mantle, tectonic
plates collide, a seam heightens, gains
     flute and pucker—and anon
          subsides, thumbed down

     by fleet
millennia as I gaze. It's young
again, the oldest young thing I know.
     A working proof
          of the axiom

of nerdy cool;
the spots blurred like black galaxies
should clash with, yet actually enhance
the crisp effect
of its mushroom gill

pinstriped tableskirt.
A train of glycerin lace tows
a collection of debris: chips
of black basalt,
the beige bells

of some
mountain flower. What if,
cooling as a cloud, a larger *I*
pores over my moraine
(the things

hitched up
to the bumper of my car,
the ball-and-chains
healed into me—)?
I pray I amuse It.

The Aerialist

I detect a busy ordering
in the corner of my eye, and catch
            dust-mote legs shuttling silk

from a diminutive abdomen, plump
as a full chignon. You float through the air, aswing
            on your trapeze, performing

a dangling ritual dance
off the temple of my glasses, then,
            swimming up, anchor me to a line

so fine I must assume
it exists, a mathematical *if/then* whose idea I ride
            to the pleated lamp shade's edge.

You rock in the gale of my breathing,
and I think of Petit, flowing
            back and forth on cable taut

between the Towers, inner ear
telegraphing to the mind the thousand
            shifts of flexing pole required

to hold his center of mass above
the dividing line, to keep spinning peril
            into joy. It would be something

to write a poem like that, whose thought
flowed like current between two
            charged points, or to sit in balance

upon a line and draw up to one
from a quarter mile below
the world's roar.

Child Acrobat

Curls float upon your shoulders, as if your baby hair
has never been cut. You smile
with shy radiance, a boy
holding something holy
in its rareness. Then your father nods
and you become the rare thing, setting the blackened sole

of your slipper in his palm, drawing up one knee
as, on the swell of three,
he tosses you aloft.
You arch your back to pour
headfirst toward us, so he can catch
your upper arm, fly you like a pennant on his mast,

your down-turned face lit by absolute trust.
Subduing the tremble of your hips
and ankles, you point
your toes like a still flame
the flesh-toned unitard has sheathed.
Your open palm sinks and rises, the balance scale

on which our childhood comes to rest, bubble fine,
having burrowed up to you in gladness
out of our flesh.
Against the branches
of the mesquite, wound round and round
in tiny stars, above the silver-greased living statues

and swallowers of fiery brands, you make us believe
only the art of the living body
begets beauty
without end. That only
what's ongoing can be perfect.
That Icarus, so long as he was falling, never fell.

The Keeper

My nephew jerks the arcing pole
to set the barb, but the hook tears
through the jaw, and the bluefish spins
on a slowing lathe—miracle alloy
of pewter and ice—

then falls between the jetty stones.
He strips off his black
Metallica T-shirt. Trembling, he reaches,
rasping his cheek on the granite boulder,
then he's got it, he cries, and hauls

it out, gripping the tail's slick sickle
through the wadded cloth.
He'd planned to let us look,
then let it go. But the jaws hitch open,
open, and cannot close.

The gills labor and flare: we watch
a bared heart heave. Gently,
the wild mechanism winds down;
the eye's capsule of golden oil goes dim.
My four-year-old asks, *Do they die*

of air? Offshore, sparkles heave
and simmer, undiminishable.
The sun sends its heat such a distance
to attach to our shoulders
its burr-like prongs. And again my father,

silver waves blown wild, gets carefully
to his knees to sluice the granite
with a bucket of brine, swirling
the sugar sand away. He pulls forward
the dorsal fin's spiny fan, pries wider

the gill slit so the kids can touch rays
of tongue-colored petals. He opens
the creamy belly, then draws out
the stomach's long nipple. He milks it,
and we all lean in to learn what it ate,

but it's puckered and slick,
a deflated balloon. He spears out
the eye, pinches its lens through the slit
to my palm. It's cloudy as a piece of hail,
and my girls touch it shyly,

rolling the moonstone over my palm's
floor, begging to keep that gem
whose water is drawn out with every touch.
The dream enters them:
that saying *I want, I want* can stay

the perishable lusters of the world.

Garnet, the Poor Man's Ruby

said the jeweler, rueful, as with a subtle
flourish of the wrist he offered back
the rose gold band on the pad
of his little finger.
And as I drew it off,
I saw how poor it was.
How a stone once worth
much labor, pulsed against the sharkskin lap
till the oval was mullioned
in burgundy wine,
could darken, could shrivel
and grow brittle like a drop of blood.

      Though she left him, my uncle kept
Julia's vanity, in whose slim drawer I found
among receipts for kerosene and carrot seed
a carmine cylinder of sweetly
chalky grease, impregnated with wood must
so it stung my throat, and this ring
he'd had engraved to her inside,
the italic *J* smudged with wear.
We had inherited his land
and all it contained,
his sheds crammed with lumber scrap
and jars of nails, the walls hung
with steel-jaw traps and coils of rope.
There was an outhouse
out of use, but still faintly redolent
of animalic soil. There was a spring
where she must have pushed a pail through
fern-etched panes of ice
to dip out water for her bath.

      The winter I was twelve, I carried pails
of water from that spring

for my horse, the goats and rabbits we kept
in a shed with a floor of dust, rat-tunneled
and shifting. Afternoons, I'd lie back
on my horse's rump as she mumbled up
her sweet feed, slipping
the ring on and off each finger,
crooning *Ju li ah* for its dove call.
Atop the prickling bales of hay
I'd hold the she-rabbit,
warming my fingers between her dewlap
and her breast. I'd run my hand along her back's
compressed spring of panic,
then embed the ring in the fold of plush
behind her ears, pretending it was
jeweler's cotton, admiring
ruby on ermine. I'd study the way
a facet, tilted right, flashed white, how
by tilting it back, I could make
the dark red juice return.
      With the ring I married me
to the Cooper's hawk I'd caught
by the shoulder of the road. A rust-streaked
tube of bone skewered
one wing. When he turned his head
at the latch's rattle, the eye
would be lit by the shaft of light
to a hemisphere of clear,
wet crimson, the glance of a being
not undone by pain, its body
its mind, enduring and omniscient.
He perched on a rafter
so erectly, fasting, though each day
I climbed the ladder to offer

liver from my palm, willing hunger
to help me tame him, stupefied
with desire for such power, such trust.
And yet my secret love
was his refusal, so pure and perfect
it lived on and on
on air. One morning I found a packet
in the dust, wrapped in rigid satin ribbons.
A tail feather caught the light
the way the flooded
furrows of a new plowed field reflect
the clouds' somber power,
snow-laden and lowering.
The talons had retracted into the down
of his breast like a clutch of onyx thorns.
When I lifted it, my hand rose
as if assisted. The gem of the eye
had punctured, and clots
fine as ant legs stitched the lids.
      I pushed a path through
marsh grass whose little rasps caught
my sleeves. My steps shattered
the webwork of ice with a wild,
clean jingle. I crouched down
and gave it to the cove's
outgoing tide, riffling a bit
like charred pages, a structure of ash
intact but fragile, rocking on low glassy waves.
When I tried to stand my lips and eyes
went numb. I had to put my forehead
to the ground until the world returned
to wash me in its wave, bringing to my eye
a stone, pale gold and flawed

with cinnamon pox. I brought
a cobble's weight upon it.
An explosion, then
a sweet smoky thread, the faded sachet
of gunpowder. And there
was garnet, the child's ruby, crazed
by the blow; a smudge of red
like a snowflake fallen on a bloody road.

Sweetbriar

My palm a wing, was it,
falling in husks of darkness
on your neck, my fingers talons stinging

you to air? Is that why you writhed
as I raised you, cool mesh
that could flow into scythe

should you will? Whose
oiled rag rubbed to such luster
your scales' ungraspable pour of sesame?

Who set those flakes of ruby
in your sides, or cauterized, then sealed
the wound's euphoria

behind pliant panes? A kink of dull
red velvet, dry-tender as a pursed lip,
is garroted between two belly scales.

It tugs my inner arm,
tags me with the odor of your inner
body, which has one meaning,

which is death.
Did the falcon's crewel hook
withdraw that loop? When you fell

out the blue, a live fife rippling,
was your belly torn on the thorn
of the sweetbriar rose

who, transpiercing, cries
I wound to heal, whose bloom
transmutes to poetry?

ii

Negative

The headlines in my blood read
        the odds of Downs had collapsed to 1 in 10.

I set the alarm to see the predawn
        meteor shower, a veil of debris
                we pass through every year,
                our atmosphere's abrasive sac
                igniting a star's
death matter. Fresh snow over the boot-tops, a day-
old crescent moon,
            Orion's belt
        a pinch of stones dropped
        and scattered, zirconia bright. In his sword
        a nebula, a blur of star nursery.

A spark glowed into being and slid across the sky,
        deliberate, needle-bright.

                In my sonogram,
the tech had moved the pointer to
        a luminous round of calcium
        in the heart, to cysts of water
in the fetal brain. *Soft markers*,
            he called them.

            Attached to you, to the idea
of you, dread regressed me:
        I watched the glittering clockwork
            of the stars and thought
                of the dusty orbits of
                riding lessons, posting the trot what seemed
            like wordless hours. My knees gripping
the piston-work.

                    So much
          expected of me, tethered
to the champion's gaze.
                              It was a relief
      to be rained out, to be allowed to spend
              the five dollar bill at the rock and mineral shop, digging
              geodes from the wooden crate to weigh
              in my hand's
      scale, the lighter
the more desirable. I'd browse baskets
of peacock ore, flashier than fuel-film
on water, Dalmation jasper, Herkimer diamonds
                                        like faceted vinegar,
                                        unworkable chips of opal
                                        vialed in mineral oil and giving
          little spits of green-blue iridescence, moss agates
like wintry pools of waterweed
                  while the owner's diamond blade
                        droned through the head I chose.
Entered, it gave
        a little vulcan sigh. Halved, its gut might glow
the neon green and magenta
              of reef fish under black light, crystals
                  fine and wetly grained as a tongue.

                    Now I was an opened world.
            The large-gauge
needle passed through my varied levels
        of resistance until, almost audibly, it breached
                  the fibrous womb. On ultrasound, a vortex
          reached a finger through the cloudy ceiling
                    toward a hummock
                        of rump and shoulders, then all went opaque,
                        the core of cyclone in a wave breaking

thunderless in me.
The doctor tugged
the balky plunger till it filled
with cloudy gold, a corpuscular ore
to be sluiced and pulped, winnowed in the centrifuge
so that x's squat-linked or languid, draping
like bows, could be untangled
and aligned in pairs
and photographed.

Wedges
of petrified wood, slices of agate dyed
gentian violet.
When I can't sleep I wander those aisles, reach
into crates for blocks swaddled
in limp newsprint,
rock candy amethyst
from Brazil, snowflake
obsidian's stilled blizzard.
Magnetite to dredge
through roadside sand till it furs itself in iron filings,
a mole's velvet.
World of ore,
of poles. Was *I*
so precarious, so trembling:
a compass needle teetering on a frictionless pin?
As *you*
were precarious:
building in me, perhaps
with some simple math awry
in the blueprints.

Your cranium of cave lakes. The comet in your heart,
its flaring coma.

At an antique mall
I'd found glass negatives wrapped in packs of five
                        in butcher paper. On the backs
            the emulsion of gelatin and silver salts
puckered like blistered skin.
            With copper tape and solder I fused
                        their edges, quicksilver chasing
            the flux which vaporized to puffs
            of sweet acidic smoke.
Though the seams were clotted, my hurricanes
            were stable. Candle-kindled,
                        a beekeeper offered up
                        the void of hive, while cloudlet
                        galaxies hovered around his head.
            Girls with sweet
            enigma mouths, with
            eye-windows for flame. I could see them
from the yard
            for I set them in the window, let them burn
                        into the night—
                                    I was afraid
                        to put you out,
my votives   *I beg of you*
            my latest altars   *Let it be negative—*

and it was,
lucid as the charge
            on an ion, a magnet's pole,
            my blood's *O negative*
                        when the doctor called and gave you back to me.

iii

Jonquil

In April, my month, my mother would push a slender vase through the belly of my cake until petals of winter butter touched the icing's glossy white. But once in early March I found a jonquil opening at the wood's edge. I thrust my hand through the tender straps, fondling the springy hollow of its stem. The sound of its plucking entered my fingers like a muffled heartbeat. I wandered the woods with the flower dying in my hand, the scent giddying me, a pain akin to hunger stretching my heart. Perhaps the stream could tell me what to do. A brittle shelf of ice, scalloped like a drawing of a cloud, grew from the edge. On this cold bed, the half-opened blossom bowed its neck while the water chuckled by. I pushed a twig through a mound of moss and inserted the stem in the bank. The inner cup made an astonished *O*, like the mouth of a minnow.

At Sunday dinner, my Nana told us the story of the jonquil. *All by its lonesome, where there weren't none before! So pretty it was against the green of the moss, so early.* I thought to own it, but didn't I know the nakedness of being stripped of wonder? And hadn't my lie made flare that belief in miracle we know as joy?

Nettles

His mildness: like dipping a hand into the soft
sweet water in the rain barrel.
He would trample a path for me
to the lone cherry tree through a lake
of nettles, dew
scattering its glass seeds
when the humid breeze parted the stalks
or flung them together again. Bearing
the pointed ladder before him
like a dowsing rod, the wooden rungs and rails
soft as balsa, grasping the hand back
like a velveted antler.
Even now, when a path takes me past
a bank of nettles, cherries
haunt my mouth. I sometimes let the leaf's teeth
graze my inner arm, so I can watch again
the whitening stings raise
their constellations, feel again
the voluptuous conscience of the skin. I've ridden
thousands of miles homeward on this leaf
whose edge I turn on my pencil's point,
observing the ampoules, each marked
with a tiny trapped lash
where the acid stops, each tipped with a glass hair
awaiting the casual touch that will explode it
like a Rupert's drop.
A young snail hugs the bristly stalk, a minute coil
the rose-rich silk of cherry bark.
The needles do no harm to its benign
and tender skirts. *They do no harm
to me*, he always said, and I thought it was because
he was so good.

Axis Mundi

and even after death you come
clearer to me as I walk a row of young trees
espaliered to wire, the graft unions
swollen near the ground where the fist of scion

grapples with the fist of rootstock
in growth's slow time.
When I asked, once, if cutting down
the old trees made you sad

you lifted your chin, closing your eyes
a moment to dismiss my unproductive line
of questioning. *All orchards*
come to need rejuvenating. Young wood bears

more heavily. Your voice is as real in my ear
as the whippoorwill calling out the dusk.
You still press upon the world, as if you are
the storm holding off, the sky spread

with a batter of cloud. I reach what is left
of the old orchard, your first planting,
Baldwins, Russets, *Good keepers.*
Heirlooms, now, spared for the moment.

Each a bonsai so magnified I can stand within
its gigantic, rugged grace.
The boughs spread their tonnage
low as benches, upholding

your judgment sixty years back
when you chose three
to train, then headed the leader off
so its ghost would open the center

to sunshine and air. Each bough
tapers to a cocked
limb, an Atlas elbow bearing up a world.
                    They bear up a world:

I lean my forehead against
a branch, its skin finely crinkled
and lichen-frilled. At my ear,
a leaf taps and lightly rasps another

with its toothed edge.
Scar radiates like the iris of an eye
around each minor wound—a water shoot
clipped off, drill of the appletree borer.

You, who loved the look
of my child's face. Who called it once
Most beautiful thing in the world, the *world*
drawn out to a caress hoarse and rich

as the tumble of gravel.
I could have told you all my metaphors
anchor here, have drunk from wounds
that trickled sap, clear,

viscous as mouthwater. Have breathed
scorched sugar as jointed limbs
smoldered on the pile, have touched,
when May awoke the trees again,

a fragrant snow, tender
and mobile.
What burns my throat when I see
in these old trees your reticence, your

forbearance? Not grief, but the compound of
dread and pity, fear
and joy, acrid as the white lead
you once painted on their wounds.

I turn and turn again; out the corner
of my eye I keep seeing
a human figure, but it's a tree split
by hurricane or the weight of its own fruit,

cut back to the dense-ringed trunk.
It's not you, yet it's all
we have left: your gradual vanishment.
Your death, going on.

Still Life with Yews

Walking to my office I had stopped
to listen   —*Where are you? where*
         are you—
A robin cast her flute notes
off a frost-blanched roof peak,
triplets ascendant,
sweetly querulous, piercing
the heart's rim, tugging through it
the long thread of music.
The world that bled back to my eye
had changed. The east had flushed
like a cheek when the cold
compress is lifted. Narcissi
lifted the gray mat of leaves.

The mind and body can be
separate places, that's what *had* and *–ing*
prove, I was thinking as I rubbed
my thumb along paper, listening to
my fingerprint's stuttering rasp. I was not turning
the page, not seeing the words, my eye
compelled to the tender green bristles
tipping the yew's black wands.
Without the aid of any wind,
they nodded; some pulse rubbed
the blood-in-milk berries along the pane.
Faint static through the glass;
the pianissimo was fading, the needle
about to lift.

And it was still the crinkle
of the paper drape I heard, the hand
outside the door, rustling through my file.

The cordial, imperturbable voice explaining
how the body mistakes
part of itself for enemy, launches cells
to kill it. That I must take a replacement
the rest of my life. My legs hung
like stopped pendulums. I was still
in that still life: mirror in its stainless frame,
Lucite jars of swabs and packaged
gauze. Propping my torso
with my hands' heels, I was nodding
like the yew outside my window, with each jet of blood
downward from the heart, into the body
that was not me, and was me.

The Sheen Remains

Better to destroy
>*outright   than to watch something*
>>*struggle   not to die*

One night that winter, I ran
>from the house as if I could outstrip
>>the front of madness, or ride it
to exhaustion, bracing with one hand
>my pregnancy's dense sphere   *better*
>>*to destroy outright than to watch*
In lit windows
>a husband pried the lid off a jar   a wife
>>ducked her chin, laughing as he cocked
a hip against the counter to gesture out
>a story   a white cat
>>tucked paws inward then sank
broodingly upon them, narrowing
>its green-gold eyes   *to watch something*
>>*struggle*   Where could I go, where could I go?

No ledge seemed spare enough
>to ghost my life except
>>the trestle above the river, cat's cradle
of iron whose rails, whetted bright,
>vibrated lightly under my hand
>>from the current or an on-bound train,
they would not tell
>*better to destroy outright than to watch*   I leaned
>>off the concrete piling, pain-pilloried, holding
one strut whose tokens of rust
>embedded my palm. Below, the swift
>>silver-membraned water

passed away. And yet
    the sheen remained, a film
        on which the moon shattered and regrouped,
melting and drawing apart
    like flame *not to die* but for all that
        whole, wholeness its essence, even as a snagged
twig tore its horizon, doubling the murmur
    to watch something struggle not to die

And I saw that everything
    I held or beheld—
        bridge, palm, moon on water, one heart
the smaller, one
    water in another, whatever remains of self
        or love—they were enough, they could support, be
supported, and though the world sang
    the submersed and airless coda
        of a dull blow *to watch something*
struggle there was a path
    through it, I could go on in my becoming.

I woke outside the window
    where he sat composed
        to destroy outright in a pool
of lamplight, reading a brilliant page.
    I thought he might look out at me
        with a night attendant's
neutral courtesy, laying down his book
    with a finger hooked inside
        to keep his place. But no, no, he couldn't
see me. I stood in the shadow
    of the house. How right with himself
        he looked, how calm in his wealth

of self, of something all his own that made
　　　the next day and the next
　　　　　a volatility, a rapture. Yet pain
awaited him too, the pain
　　　that for a time becomes our all. Let something else
　　　　　bring it home to him.

Then what could I wound? The snow was old,
　　　the earth rigid and dumb. She gave and gave.
　　　　　She would forgive me for beating her side
with a length of wood until
　　　numbness climbed from palm to tongue,
　　　　　for stretching out upon her like the dead.

The Flash Phenomenon

*Despite her father's refusal to grant her a formal education, Lisa Stina
Linnaeus (1743-1782) wrote a paper called "The Gaze of the Nasturtium"
for the Royal Swedish Academy of Sciences. Flourescence in the nasturtium's
petals causes some people to see a flash of light, particularly at twilight, just
as they turn their eyes away.*

Her braids have resumed the flossy nap
     of ripening barley. She darts from the barn
         like a lark or a swift, a bird
    always on wing. Her sisters teach
father's apostles—baronets'

second sons, ship's doctors in training—
     the *vals* and *polska* by mime,
         raising the men's
    plant-stained palms to waists
whose ruffles and floral brocade disguise

the framework of bone stays. She cannot explain
     the figures of the dance. French
         is forbidden, though her half-fingered
    gloves were tatted in a convent near
Rouen. And Latin, too, though its sound is

familiar as the hand-pump's gush
     over cobbles. She holds those words
         her deepest known, unfettered
    by sense, the way she owns the spiraled
and chalky halls of her father's conchs,

and the sea inside. Catching her breath
     on the arbor's bench, she finds the midnight sun
         pooling fire at the roots of hilltop pines, still
    casting light enough for the dial to figure the hour
on raked gravel. Her feet are lost in leaves

of large coinage, star-sapphire veined,
        and blossoms whose ruched hems
            glow intense as blown coals.
        Their gates narrow to a darkness
of interlocking plush,

a sweet enforcement the bees stagger
        to emerge from, drunk with fumbling.
            The flowers hypnotize
        her sight, dilating like pupils to delve as deep
into her blood as the almost-kiss

that could not be. Turning her neck to break
        their gaze, she sees the flash that will take
            her name, rupturing the mind's calm night.
        It's the moment her father held
an ember to the wick trailing from

the cunningly folded lily. No, it's after.
        After the greedy bee sizzles toward
            the nugget of salts and metals,
        when, with a gasping flare,
petals birth star-fire.

Study with Bark, Stones, Leaves, and Mother

The spackled-on husks
of the hemlock. Soft gloss on the oak treads
as if splashed with melted wax.
Even in the mica gloom of the middle woods
trunks whiten like erasures.
The sun reaches in, abrades to the paper.
My mother's hair, long as it was
when I was a girl, bewilders my eyes like snow.
The blue-tinged white of gesso.
Her snowy egret stillness.
She crouches on the shore, pressing
a nub of stone with her thumb
until it slips from its socket. She grips
to feel what tool it is, could be.
Her favorites she's packed close as mussels
in the cleft of a boulder so the cove
can't reclaim them, so she can go on
attending them, be present when they speak.
Slants of sun come up beneath
the beech leaves, illuminating
the emerald screens. Whereas when two
leaves lap, green absolutes to black.
Oak leaves putty-colored, the muddied water
in the watercolorist's glass. The arcing
flutter of the beech leaves, the oak leaves
clapping their vellums.
*What's going through that mind
of yours*, I ask as she stands
to stretch her back.
The wing of the snowy egret grazes
the dissolving verge of the day moon and
its evening power
comes on, the oyster-shell radiance. *I was thinking—
I was thinking how like figures we are
in a painter's landscape.*

The Model Plane

Uppland, Sweden

I climb past farms, once inns named
  Distress and Suffering. Then,
     at the turn, there's Joy, where two girls
        tuck ducklings like buttercups

beneath their chins. Pillar clouds glide,
  their dense gray pediments
     borne on some transparent palm
        of pressure. The sky's a deep

delphinium blue. The pelt of wheat
  goes sleek and pale, is carded
     darkly back in buffets
        of wind. And I see

what I've been hearing
  downhill, round-the-bend.
     A brassy buzz unmuzzled, out
        of clouds. A toy plane spirals

toward the field, tethered on a hair-
  of-glass radio wave. A foot above,
     the nimble pullout, skim-and-roll:
        leisurely blink of red, then white,

then red. The nose rises, drills straight up—
  the motor's thinning
     whine a valiant
        little sound—then, shoulder over, plunge.

Over and over for the boy in a red shirt.

Trick the Eye

"Deceptions and Illusions: Five Centuries of Trompe l'Oeil Painting,"
National Gallery, Washington, D.C., 2003

1.

Deceptions and Illusions

We shifted our weight from foot to foot,
bags held to our chests like infants
at a clinic and offered to the bored attendant
who probed the contents
    with a tapered wooden wand,
        who patted us down
            with brisk abstracted palms.
              Then my husband
    and I trundled the props of happy family life—
Sippicup, stroller, toddler—
through the metal-detecting arch
and the green light
blinked us aboard the exhibit.
    Where high windowed arcades
        sword-pierced with sunrays
            telescoped from zinc-white galleries.
            Where parquetry glazy as honey
        lured the eye through Gothic arches
            hung with gilt-caged finches.
    We turned corners
  where no corners were
to follow a line of veiny urns
cascading ivy. Drawn by the arm
of potted palms embracing
    a reflecting pool dappled with silver bullion,
    we came upon an emblem
        of unearthly peace:
    from a marble terrace
        floating like a stage

we viewed the peacock tray
of sea, a scimitar of golden sand,
and, half-lost to us in the violet
fume of distance, a dove-gray ass
harnessed to a plow
      no larger than a thorn
           turning a furrow
                at the foot of the volcano.

2.

Temptation for the Hand

My daughter froze before a silver
Persian bunkered to outlast
      the siege of her gaze
           behind the slats of a crate
knotholed like a slice of Emmenthaler.
Alarmed, green-marble-eyed, the cat
      displayed wet needles, a bristled
           griffin's tongue cupped to hiss,
so her hovering finger withdrew
from the pelt's allure.

Though the hand touched a flat surface,
           the eye, still seduced, saw relief.
My husband, urged by an oddly solicitous
      guard to thumb to page so-and-so
of the catalogue and blow his mind
on the *bomb dot com* of surrealism
      jerked fingers back from the book jacket
           decoupaged on plywood, shocked—
then placed his palm down
firmly, finger pads mapping out

the force field that banned him from
that volume.

        I gazed longest at
a ghost clock, the pleats
      in its cord-cinched dust sheet
        crisply classical, even
as the strings on a lyre. Not
the unknowable, not god,
      but a gaunt tower whose hem I'd knelt
    to in dreams, kissed to find
the cloth implacable, mahogany-cold:
the mind in its surgical gown
         about to bring the patient round,
    having stripped whatever cataract
lets the heart
not see what it sees, not know
  what it knows.

3.
Niches, Cupboards, and Cabinets

The image I chose to hover
in the void of my first book's cover
    suddenly expanded to arrest me:
    Remps' *Cabinet of Curiosities*,
one glass door invitingly ajar
    but cracked, wet light riding
the fractures. Near to hand, intaglios
and cameos.
        Venous coral taut with blood.
        A meteorite's cratered ore. A crystal globe's
          moony glow. A convex mirror in whose curve
there seemed to lurk an iris, contemplative
yet alien   *No pupil! And so sealed from us*
And sterile—   And inhuman (our speculations nesting
        nicely, then off on a wing)
Must be why modern sculptors
gouge them in—   Why the pressed sugar arcs
of Grecian eyes repel us—
        Though they're beautiful
        And a hollow, lathe-turned bauble
    spiked like a battle mace, through whose pupil-
hole one could spy
        a Habsburg icon on an inch of bone,
          or a miniaturized War of Roses
    pageantry, or gladiators jousting
in a dollhouse coliseum...
        Milling folks, we made a battened
ear-plugged din, suspended gratefully
        in the game of make-believe
    where things are only
what they seem, where nothing seems
        as broken as it. We could forget for now
        what lay beyond
    the sound-proofed
        walls: the orange alert, troop movers
          flying low and slow over the city, the snipers'
    cushioned footfalls on the roof.

Zebra Finch at Petco

The male tweezes a bald millet stalk
off the sahara of graveled paper.

The pert watch movements of his head
ignite an ember on each cheek, buff bright

the beak's rose-hip hue. His elderberry eye
subjects this meter cubed of universe

to further scrutiny. The struggles of
a downy filament attract him.

With these two finds he alights, caresses
the injection-molded branch. But there is

no flaw to catch on, no way to make a start.
A problem he sets aside for the moment,

pinning it down with his foot. In the dusky
corner his mate dangles from brass wires,

mobile as a chandelier earring.
Extending her wing, she makes him

more to find, fussing
a small snow from the hot and pearly hollow.

iv

Salvage

i.

We're safe giving grief of any kind
　　or scale to something

　　so mutable
where trees compromise with the current's

undercut of bank by growing out
　　narrow docks

　　leaf-awninged
over the water. So full of digression, so able

to reclaim our prosaic trash—scummed
　　and rainbow-faded

　　a Cheer jug bashed
to brittle shard, mulch fabric

bunched in tree crotches, scraps of raft
　　snagged ten feet up a tree.

　　A scene enduring, no, enriched
by calamity, velveted anew

each flood in silt. Stress can make beautiful
　　what suffering lets go of.

　　The slick transcript I'd made
of his desire for another, not for me,

I'd stumbled on, then
　　hoarded until got by heart

I tore to
strips, then luminous rungs

~ give yourself ~

~ how I wish ~

~ in one ~

that spun their origami moment

~ I only know I am in ~

~ such risks ~

~ the courage to insist ~

extended their wings,
     their euphoria subdued, somehow

     more moving. It was
possible to confess I had envied, had

admired them
     as they drank to a waxed transparency

     as they sank
to petals, radium green.

ii.

Three days rain   so altered
the mobile verge   the evidence
I'd unpossessed   was
doubly hidden
Even the place I'd crouched   had drowned
in that spacious bed

The river takes   all our sadness or offense
without reproach   like a girl
her hymen torn   coming to her door to lean
her cheek against   the frame   lower lids sooted
sleep   smutched   under lip
with the   should-have-been-adored
freckle in its border

This river
has her eyes

iii.

When my walks had turned to blind staggering
in the wastes of our estrangement, the river threw

its lifeline to my eye. On the bank, low leaves
netted with light, a pagoda of yellow petals,

a stem arched just so that tremble could go on:
the trout lily, and not just one,

no, one linked others to my eye, nodding,
pointing with their chins

Look

                   there is still a world

out here   even if pain
               has made you stupid.

iv.

I walk the trunk out over the water, my steps
        shuddering schools

of silver-bellied leaves. I hold to vertical
        branches jointed as the hard legs of horses

and look down at the cursive of snail trail,
        the counterclockwise of minnows that keep

a place by acceding to a new one,
        a lanky waterweed tumbling through

a tangle of branches. In the shallows
        a carp flops its sunning self,

then shoots off, a muscular kick conducting
        to my chest the volts of animal alarm.

Herds of beetles, featureless
        as drops of hot solder, zoom

and slalom along the surface, colliding
        like electrons, taking momentum from that push.

A view's made possible by a bearable
        duress, by roots feeling out

what anchorage there is within a shifting bank.
Whatever happens

becomes part of this beauty, will be incorporated
in the growth pattern over time.

Pear Tree

The scale had finally tipped. The crown
had leant the trunk's coarse twist
too far, had torn the root
from the earth's socket. Rain moistened
the dry rot into marrow, a paste
of henna coating the frayed tongue.
Yet the bud-pearls
went on loosening, day by day whitening
the twig wood. Perhaps
it could still drink the rain.
Perhaps sap rises and rises its fill
like a tide, pulled by the novae of transient stars.
Winter rye grew tall between the branches.
Each day I chewed
one rasping blade, folding it greedily
into my mouth. The sweet juice foaming,
stinging my throat.
Today I stood before a tissue of sunlight, behind which
the gilt cage burned. Sparks
lifted off it, or drifted fading down.
I stepped inside,
and the wail of bees rose around me.
I stood; they knocked against me, settling
their squirming burrs on my hair.
I have no flowers for you, I said
and crossed through that veil.

Imago

Io Moth

Because it confined us
outside its patent-slick capsule,
because no mortal eye can bear witness
to change gradual as it is wondrous,
we'd lost interest in the miracle on our sill.
How long ago the burgundy hooks
embedded their stitches in the laurel leaf
is anyone's guess. That lean-to's
gone auburn, propped weeks ago
inside the sheer-walled oubliette.

We pet the forehead, high-domed
as a day-old kitten's. The antennae
shiver so exquisitely we expect the vanes,
mimosa-like, to fold. Nudging our finger
along the edge of the wing
tautens the abdomen to the leaf. Tightens
the tongue's coil to a tiny coin
in the plush breast.
Pearlescent minerals come off on our fingers.
The forewings swag like curtains
above a stage. We absorb the set design:
out a hollow like the mouth
on a mask of tragedy
an owl gazes, pupils banded
in bullion gold. And in the absolute black
of each telescope field,
the coarse cheek of an old, flawed pearl,
the dwindling memento of our world.
Our hair stirs in the silent draft
of wings. As if it is Clio, muse of history,
launching from the throat of the noble oak,
never to return,

never to tell us how she fit
all those tapestries and ancient maps
in such a small scroll.

Do You Breathe?

Transfixed beneath five mannequins
in bikinis and sarongs, it was breath
she watched them for, reaching to touch
a plaster arch, a prima-donna toe impaled
by an aluminum rod. *Does breathing move it*?
She eyed the breasts, air-brushed bronze

and gravity proof as pyramids.
          Standing back, I registered the scale
of things: the volume of air overhead, cube
windows at ceiling height, repeating
Roman numeral fives of supporting trusses.
Yards-long buzzing tubes of fluorescence shed

a fine dry snow on her black hair
as she looked up into giant Barbie faces,
into eyes cast so deep the cinnamon brows
threw slate shadows on the blue
unblinking pools.
                      I've come across

the afterlives of mannequins, have held
my breath to ask them *do you breathe*:
a scarecrow in Missouri corn, hospice-
patient-bald and thin under a housedress
fluttering like surrender's makeshift flag.
Or in a hunter's blind, conditioning

the mallard to see stillness as the essential
human aspect, hair stiff as straw under
the army-surplus cap. One headless, hung
by a leg from the frathouse portico, graffiti'd
ANONYMOUS HOLE in red spray.
                Further back,

the coma girl who shared my name,
and slept slit-eyed while the iron lung
pushed air in her, birthing in me a dread of dolls
whose hinged and weighted lids
could rise when they were tilted, revealing
pupils bottomless as mine shafts.

Now she sleeps at my breast, smiling in dream,
lightly breathing around me, and I think
I will remember you this way always, sound
and slackly warm, hair damp at the crown
where I feel for the fontanelle that allowed
her passage through me, and had nearly closed.

Obeisance

He was lean. Streaked with grease to his shoulders.
He had a lank, loose-gathered ponytail. A face
grimed with asphalt dust out of which
the milk-blue eye whites stared. Eyes
of someone living with bad news, or himself
bad news, or simply famished.

My mother let him in while my father was at school.
Something to do with
a broke-down truck, the phone, a sandwich? The shower:
the sound of falling water, steam curling out
the half-opened door, the wallpaper with silver eagles perched
in federal pose. I'm coming closer,
closer. The powder blue porcelain sink.
A glimpse of jeans, the legs
the oily gold of eel skins, draping
the edge. Do I imagine this now
or was I there? Did I watch him
step out of the shower through the hinge-gap
of the door, did he want me to see his nudity?
He placed his palm
over the stiffening, hooked fingers over the head to hold
it downward and away. How else could I see this? How else
could I know?

My mother has no memory of him.

He kaleidoscopes with other dark men
of my childhood, the one who tried to sell me
green coconuts for quarters on the beach in Florida,
jean cutoffs unraveling in fringes to his knees,
shoulders seared to oxblood, eyes
all pupil like a clubbed animal's. Or

the rosewood Jesus in Nana's hall, eyes rolled
upward, bodyweight thinning
the chest fleshless, the belly's shallow bowl
between hip bones straining up
like the wings of a taunted swan. My uncle,
paralyzed in a dim room, his neck
arching back to keep his head upon
the pillow, slipping on the black hair, luxuriant and coarse, over
and over like a man treading water with his last strength.

That gesture. Like the little female cat, a brown-tufted black who,
brain-tumor-driven, turned in place
with a compulsive grace so intent it seemed sexual.
An obeisance: like kneeling before
your god. Her low-slung belly bulged
with knobby fruit. She dropped each of her
five kittens in a different province
of my childhood. Under the boathouse
where black crickets bred, in the wild mustard
behind the sand pile. In the storm drain that traveled under
the steep yard like a throat,
by the blacksnake hole in plush moss where toadstools spread
their ruby cowls. One near-far we sought
under bittersweet vines, in the chokecherries, until its shrill
hunger-cries wavered, then went silent. Covered
in something—lice, maggots?—we shampooed
them in that sink, briar-claws catching on flaws
in the pale blue glaze,
fur clumped in points like wet lashes.

He was dirty, and thin, his face a mask of grease which white eyes
hollowed. She let him in while my father was at work.
I would go to the bathroom, after, open the closet, finger

the satin-covered buttons on her garter belt, work
her eyelash curler, clamping its gummed lids.

Did I cry out and no one came? Is this why I can't bring myself
to pray to God? He held himself, then slyly
showed the head to me, as if to say
I'll teach you to love the men who frighten you.

Prudence

Foolhardy, late-blooming sweet pea, skirts
wilted to one tissue from the frost. I thought
you might be good to eat, as some
flowers are. A taper of sunlight warmed you
and you stood again. I beckoned you in.
You felt the walls of brushed earth
with your fingertips. No rootling
so pale or fine. All that spring and summer
you were grateful, knitting me silk
of the spider's web, sweeping
pollen off my back with the teasel brush.
While we sorted barley from rye
you sang me tales of gypsy rovers, galleons,
of queens arrayed in cloth of gold. I wanted
to keep you, teach you to put value in the heart
of the labyrinth: the storeroom
and the hoard. But you had more feeling for
worn-out creatures, for the thriftless
and improvident who do not deserve
to live—the swallow so taken with
his lavish flight he did not smell
the coming snow. You stole felts of wool I'd gleaned
from the pediments of graves
to blanket him, as if his beauty
should exempt him from death's coldness.
I was watching. I saw you kiss
his half-open eyes.
There's something indecent in that.
I am the one who saved you and I'll trade you
as I will. I choose to give you to
the earth-shouldering mole
whose pelt is denser than a cattail's,
whose torso is packed as the pod

of the still-green milkweed. He loves
delicate things, though he cannot fondle them
with his outward-facing palms. But they are rich
with folds, like walnut meats, and generous.
It was cruel of you to say
his eye glitters like a flytrap's dew. Can he help
that light is death to him?
How would it harm you to press
your flawless bosom to his breast, or lace
your tresses through the fingers
of his starnose?

Pessary

(n.) A device inserted into the vagina to support the uterus.

It's a wild boar, ventures a friend,
duped by the dactyl *peccary*, while to me
    sheer euphony suggests
the voile wound in an X
    to lift and separate
damsel breasts or *a garment*
    undergirding chastity or how about
a rosary of semi-precious stones
    pinned to a nun's hip.

    I'm close: the root's
the Greek *pessos*, "oval pebble,"
    attesting that we've always used
the near-to-hand to stopper up
    that hole. Like the elderly woman
who complained of
    growths from the privates,
and revealed when in stirrups
    a literal cascade
of green shoots—the jointed, antennal
    potato eyes seeking light, leaf-tipped,
stirred out of dormancy by the richly
    folded moisture of their root cellar.
Who's grubbed potatoes from a row
    and not mistaken
stone for staple, for earth apple?

    Didn't her mother once admire
what she'd made, the baby labia
    faintly puckered on inner edge like
clementine membranes, and the way

they clung to the adorable
pale coral of the hood? Hadn't a lover
        once muttered through the bars
of shielding fingers, begging to tongue
        the blood flush there, to taste
alarms set firing along nerve ends
        wild with surprise?

Poor vault, prolapsed to a womb chute
        by our most binding contract,
into and out of which
        we come, poor fallen shrine.
Where is your sacristan now?

Something Hard Under the Skin

In a flash she is my total love again
as she kneels on the bed, skin
humid from the bath, her small waist
creasing at the hip with a melting sweetness.
Her mouth returns to its infant
sorrow pout, lips thinned as she tastes
the hollow of air that will become
the fretful sob, the half-cough I remember
when she clamored for
the slackening and oblivion
at my breast. *I don't
want to change*, she cries, covering with her palm
the blue-black strands between her legs, crimped
as lambswool filaments. *Now there's something
hard under the skin* and she brings
my finger to her nipple
with both hands.
Once she entrusted to my palm
a leafy twig with a small plum healed
to a larger, begging me not to break
the baby from its side.
Now she is torn from me
as the estrogenic flood rises
in her blood, just as mine
quiets and descends. I watch from the bank.
Her chaste body composes itself
to be broken, to ride through the market
with slender, swaying shoulders.
She pulls her damp hair forward, hugs to her chest
Godiva's cape, covering those pearls
that rise under the skin.

Surrogate

It fell—it fell from the sky—the nest—
they clamor hoarsely. My older girl unfurls
her hand, reveals an egg the same faint blue
of the day moon, dull as frost and flawless
as a Jordan almond. Then holds the cell
to her ear. *I think I hear it cry.*

—o—

First a fracture in the egg's parabola,
then a flap thrown back, hinged with milky skin.
A cheep, subtle as a walled-up cricket's.
Something strains and shifts, chiseling out that peephole.
Slow-motion-sick, we watch as it revolves and winds
itself in kinked, yolk-stiffened down.

—o—

Stranded on the heating pad, all day it croons
a podcast of progress to the brooding Beyond.
The girl attunes her ear to it, becomes
its mother, hovering all day to watch the puncture
widen to an aperture in cloud-cover
over an empurpled, wrinkled continent.

—o—

Nothing simpler or more terrible: the head
jigging on a spring, the beak exploding
at a touch like a touch-me-not seedpod.
The metallic chirp chills my heart like a notice
of default, or the *mayday* of the run-down
battery in the attic smoke alarm.

—o—

On its grin, a smear of blood where my tweezers
nicked the yellow bumpers. By noon
a scrotum of flies and wormlings dangled
off its breast. The eyes were blueberries
sealed in phyllo. The stubby wings
were livid pink and cocked like fetal thumbs.

—o—

I tried to emulate the mother's brisk de-winging, to pluck
off parts too crisp or sharp. But the playground
bully's song came back—*baldy, baldy*—pure tenor notes
mocking the sockets where the grasshopper's
capes and thighs attached. That stoic oval stare
came back: I held a paraplegic in my palm.

—o—

My daughters grieve as we return the hatchling
to the alley, setting the willow basket down
under a gorgon tree, a crux of black
sheathed power cables running down
a galvanized trunk to enter New Morning Bakery.
Fear and failure delivered fresh daily! the brash world avows.

—o—

We back away. Above, reedy feeding calls;
below, the sharp, single-minded beacon. Something
flutter-tumbles like a clod of dust, refines to a swoop:
the sparrow perches, runs some feathers through her beak
to zip them tight. She cocks her head, sedately
hones her beak, and listens at the basket's brink.

Exchange of Azalea and Quail

Something special you're wanting?

I'd a vision of a white azalea,
a crown to hover
     like a spreading oak's above the mound
I'd made, around which curved
     a bark path's rustic valley.

          Aye, true dwarf,
though that don't keep
     the bobwhite quail setting
her clutch beneath it.

     Size and heat
of shooter marbles left in the sun.

     Don't never see the mother go,
but she's always off the nest
     when he comes down the row.

Now, yesterday he felt nothing
     but a bit of shell. So he stepped
full weight on the shovel, leaned back
     to rock the root ball free, when up
boiled the shrub like a pan of milk, the chicks
     a clump he could've picked up
all at once.

     Ball of cockleburs
they was.

     Minute he got a finger on
they burst apart, tunneled
     like voles in the tall grass,

said the nurseryman, the boyish shock
    of tawny-silver bangs falling
across one candid eye as he set
    my azalea in the trunk.

To the Ox Netsuke in the Flea Market

You captured light, keeping some,
letting some go, alive as cartilage.
The hand the idea of you amused

fused porcine to bovine, ovine
to piscine, capping the gadfly-
maddened tossing head

with a snout's wooden spool,
planting a horn meek
as a sheep's teat inside each ear's

ragged cabbage leaf, dangling
an earlobe of dewlap
off the neck slick as a fingerling trout.

If I had held you shell-like to my ear
I might have caught
your maker ruminating:

commiseration whispering with delight.
Instead, I fell for you, one of the many
pettiness detectors

that booby-trap our world.
For the cloven toes on your left hind hoof
had fractured off, and the face

those absent noses left
was coarse as emery. That's all it took
to make me put you down, to

disenamor me.
To keep me from being
the better person who took you home.

Sutures

The woman on the other side
of emergency's curtain groaned
my babies   my babies
as a muffled voice imparted
the bad news, and I saw beyond the hem

the blunt hands of her feet
clinging and rubbing, gray heels
cracked like neglected dough, ankles
traversed by puffy rivers, while
on our side with tender precision

the doctor dipped the curved needle
to close the curtain on
my toddler's skull, setting to the side
tremulous sympathy
as the small body called urgently

for repair. My love could not
help it. When I raised
the corner of the towel
lead-heavy with her blood and saw
gold seed-pearls of fat, and beneath them

the clean edges of her meat
opening on the bluish skull, gleaming
like plastic, my body had urged me
to cover the wound's lips
with my lips   *flesh of my flesh* as if I could be

a human suture beyond the needs
of food or water, speech or air.
              Her face was draped and cross-
draped in blue. I had access only to
one fixed and anxious eye, so I whispered

into its dark unfurnished room
our next day's trip to my childhood
home, setting afloat
a boat with a green and yellow sail, reaching
her hand into leaves

for the peaches she could pick
and eat.
              Where is this paradise
our doctor murmured while she laid
a track with filament so fine
the wrists revolving, throwing loops

for glinting tools to shoot through,
seemed pure pantomime. And yet
the wound drew closed
as I watched, obeying those intricate
continuous knots.

The Bridge

For my father

A confectionary fragrance, bland and fine,
        flows over my lounge. Sweet Betty,
                I think, the pale pink
drawstring purses blooming with their feet in brine.
        Bleached straps of shore grass
                turn light buffets of wind
to extravagant crackling.

A band of cirrus plates
        the sun's disk platinum.
                And still it smarts
the eye, inclines it to idle, drowse.
        A crinkle of wavelets wakes me.
                The Sunfish has given the dock
the slip. The sail doubles over, slithers

on itself, then a rope's snubbed tight
        and the cheek fills with wind, goes translucent
                as a bubble on milk. My family, three
life-vested stumps (small, smaller,
        tiny), is shooting now
                between the footings of the bridge,
now stalled in its clangor and blotted up

in shade. Where a cement truck
        rumbles, the tilted white capsule
                with great stateliness revolving;
where weekenders up from Yonkers or Jersey bounce on reggae's
        loose suspension, prop sunburned ankles
                on the side-view mirror, while behind them
the rider of a mechanical yellow-jacket

drops a gear and opens throttle.
       Revving the engine to a nasal whine,
          he rises—he is riding the span on
the fat back tire, an oily flag of hair
       flapping to tatters behind him!
          I should mind it, yet I rather like it,
this conduit above the cove: business, leisure, risks

distracting me, sweetening my freedom, sharpening
       my alarm when the boat
          appears beyond it in the sun,
acutely tilted, seized by a body
       of westerly wind. A hand fine as a tentacle
          grasps the tiller. I know
what it feels: the keel's tingle as it scrubs

through water, how the groan
       ascends by half-steps to a song, how the song
          vibrates your palm as you part
schools of herring, or drive on the shiners
       to leap and scatter
          snips of fresh silver
over the bow wave.

The Birthday

The wild mum's violet petals
    cringe inward like a touched
    anemone as a flame from
the candle we've embedded
        in the glazy custard of your tart
does a scare dance on the vase's globe, and
the cranberry wax fogs over
          as if perspiring. We are all
    shy with wonder, giggling

and giddy, shuddering in first plunge
    of chill water as you show us
    how to pass
a finger through the flame.
      We shiver because two
charismata meet, both
with the power to destroy. You mock the flame
      as you've mocked
    us all, pranking yet tender,

assured of possession. The truth is
    you're in thrall to us and so you need
    to make us feel at once
our beauty and our foolishness. *See, hold*
      your palm above it and YAH!
But pass your finger quickly through
it . . . and here your finger gives
      the flame a few brisk slaps,
    kid glove to an insubordinate cheek. The flame

winces then stretches back
    taller than before, and again
    you smart it, curling your forefinger
round its neck like
        a shepherd's crook to pull it off
its stage. The lip of flame quivers
    as we all take turns, even
        little Lily, her squeals
    of bravado bolstered to aplomb,

sniffing her finger for its sheath
    of soot.
    Angel-beautiful, flowing
in an upward stream,
        the flame set dancing in all
your eye-lights bends
    and parts where I touch it, draws up
        again healed and whole.
    Love, deal gently with us.

Notes

About the title: in many cultures and religions, the *axis mundi* is a point of contact where the upper and the lower worlds meet, often symbolized as a tree, mountain, tower, or steeple. It is also associated with the umbilicus, and with male and female sexuality. The *axis mundi* ultimately evokes home, the concentration of all we value, our holdfast in the world.

"Ward" was written in response to a photograph of a mother finding her drowned child on the beach, after the 2004 Indian Ocean Tsunami.

"The Aerialist" was inspired by the French high wire artist Philippe Petit, who walked a tightrope between the Twin Towers at 7 a.m. on August 7, 1974.

"Sweetbriar": in Victorian floriography, the sweetbriar rose has two meanings, *I wound to heal,* and *poetry.*

"Nettles" refers to the Rupert's drop, a teardrop-shaped body of blown glass whose surface tension is so strong, one can smash the drop with a hammer and not break it. However, if one snaps off the thread of glass at its tip, the drop will fracture explosively into shards fine as sand.

"Axis Mundi" remembers my grandfather, Harold Holmberg.

"Trick the Eye": The titles of sections 2 and 3 were taken from specific "rooms" of the exhibit. Two lines of "Temptation for the Hand" ("Though the hand touched a flat surface...") are by Denis Diderot. The artworks reflected on here include S.S. David's *Cat in a Crate* and Wendell Castle's *Ghost Clock*, which is carved from a solid block of mahogany. The left margin of "Niches, Cupboards, and Cabinets" is modeled on the pre-9/11 Manhattan skyline.

"Salvage" is set on the banks of the Susquehanna River, in central Pennsylvania.

"Obeisance" was influenced by Freud's concept of the *screen memory*, in which an early memory—sometimes fabricated—serves as a screen for a later, more disturbing event.

I'm indebted to Julie Long for the anecdote at the heart of "Pessary."

Karen Holmberg won the Vassar Miller Prize for her book *The Perseids: Poems*. Her poems and essays have appeared in *Southern Poetry Review, Slate, The Nation, New England Review,* and elsewhere. Influenced by a biologist father, she is interested in science, medicine, and the natural world. She received her PhD in English (poetry) at the University of Missouri in Columbia. She currently directs the MFA program at Oregon State University and lives in Corvallis, Oregon, with her husband and two daughters.